Bygone Merseyside

1. Parry's toy shop, by Chorley Court (*right*), in Dale Street c1900. Imagine the prices that these toys would fetch today! Note the big tin trunks.

Derek Whale

First Published 1989 by
Archive Publications Ltd
Carrington Business Park
Urmston
Manchester M31 4DD
in association with
The Liverpool Echo
P O Box 48
Old Hall Street
Liverpool L69 3EB

Printed and bound in the United Kingdom by
Netherwood Dalton & Co Ltd, Huddersfield

ISBN: 0-948946-44-X

2. Roseberry Street residents celebrate winning the first prize in Liverpool's Charter Year Street Decorations
Competition, June 1957.

Introduction

Liverpool — Britain's most exciting city outside of London! That is how growing numbers of tourists are now regarding this rapidly-changing Merseyside jewel — and for good reasons. It is a friendly seaport city, acclaimed throughout the world for song and laughter, with a maritime and commercial history unsurpassed.

Once honoured as the Second City of the British Empire, it boasts a wealth of interest in many fields. Liverpool was home to some of the world's finest luxury liners and other famous ships in its heyday, and it is still the nearest deep-sea port to America, with ultra-modern northern docks. Perhaps through its cosmopolitan population, chiefly comprising English, Irish, Welsh and Scots who have settled here over the centuries, Liverpool is noted for its spontaneous hospitality and rich humour.

Although parts of Merseyside embrace communities still retaining Lancashire accents, Liverpool virtually stands alone with its own renowned 'Scouse' accent. There is a tremendous fund of goodwill and affection for this city and its people throughout the world.

Liverpool's relatively high proportion of those with Irish ancestry stems from Ireland's potato famine of the 1840s, when some 300,000 from the north as well as the south of that country crossed the sea to Liverpool, hoping to obtain passages to the New World and seek pastures new. Thousands of them, however, with little or no cash and possessions, settled in Liverpool. Between 1830 and 1930, more than 9,000,000 emigrants passed through the Port of Liverpool — not to mention thousands more since then, including GI Brides!

The Port of Liverpool continues to play an important role in the commerce of Britain and, in time of war, it has served as a most vital factor in the well-being and defence of the country. In the last war, it was the headquarters for the Battle of the Atlantic — a battle which, had it been lost, undoubtedly would have left Britain at the mercy of the enemy. Small wonder that Liverpool was the most heavily bombed area in the Provinces.

Liverpool is the birthplace of so many great achievements and prominent people. Its fame in the divisions of shipping, commerce, academic research, music and humour are renowned. Do the Beatles and so many other top groups from hereabouts need an introduction? Ask the thousands of visitors from abroad who make this 'Beatleland' their first port of call!

Who, in Britain certainly, has not heard of laughter-makers like Tommy Handley, Arthur Askey, Rob Wilton, Ted Ray, Ken Dodd, Tom O'Connor, Jimmy Tarbuck and Stan Boardman . . .? And other entertainers, like Frankie Vaughan, Derek Guyler, Rex Harrison, Ann Ziegler, John Gregson, the McGann Brothers, Cilla Black, Faith Brown, Gerry Marsden, Leonard Rossiter . . . and playwrights and scriptwriters, including Alan Bleasedale, Willy Russell, Carla Lane, Beryl Bainbridge and the late-lamented radio presenter Ray Moore?

On perhaps a more serious note, the Royal Philharmonic Orchestra, founded as the Liverpool Philharmonic Society in 1840, has no peer in the world of music.

The city's two mighty football clubs, Liverpool and Everton, need no introducing, either. Each has a long and successful history and have fielded between them illustrious players like the legendary 'Dixie' Dean, Tommy Lawton, Billy Liddell, Joe Mercer, Kenny Dalglish, Roger Hunt, Kevin Keegan, Alex Young, Brian Labone, Graeme Souness, Neville Southall and Ian Rush.

Today, much of Liverpool's riverside, originally embracing some seven miles of docks and warehouses that stored the riches of the world, is steadily changing purpose and design. Many of the port's ancient, moribund docks are undergoing dramatic redevelopment.

The massive development of the Royal Seaforth Docks, at the estuarial end of the Mersey, incorporates vast container, grain and timber terminals, and the new 600-acre Freeport is the largest and most successful one in Britain.

How many cities can boast of being virtually a seaside resort, too? Liverpool is now well on the way to creating its own waterfront resort and already boasts magnificent riverside gardens, parkland and a long promenade.

Also, hundreds of acres of formerly derelict docks and warehouses are being transformed into one of the finest water-sports playgrounds and entertainment centres in the country.

The conversion projects for Liverpool's South Docks and the construction of the Festival Gardens have proved not only wonderful and imaginative feats that are a credit to the nation, but have laid the foundation for a completely new-look Liverpool.

Under the direction of the Merseyside Development Corporation, established by the government in 1981, some 850 acres of formerly derelict docks and waterfront land are being transformed into picturesque regions with centres of entertainment, shopping, business and housing.

A major job in this respect was that of preparing 250 acres of 'badland' — oil-storage tanks, decayed buildings and rubble — into the site which became the glorious International Garden Festival, opened by the Queen in 1984.

This prestigious event was a great honour for Liverpool, although the tight deadline for its completion made the task seem impossible at first. But Liverpool made it — a vast, flower-filled, colourful jig-saw of botanical showpieces from countries all over the world.

Brilliant planning, unabated hard work in all weather and a grim determination to finish the job waved the wand that transformed that depressing region into a riverside setting of great beauty. It became the country's biggest tourist attraction, pulling in nearly 3.5 million visitors.

The magnificent Albert Dock complex, now Liverpool's most popular attraction, is yet another marvellous aspect of the changing face of Liverpool. But before this project is revealed, let us pause and find out how Liverpool and its massive array of docks came into being....

It is hard to believe that this great city and port grew from a tiny fishing village and a tidal creek called the 'Pool', on the bank of the deep and fast-flowing Mersey.

Not even the Romans foresaw the geographical possibilties of this little haven. They simply passed it by. But wise King John estimated its importance and potential as a port and, indeed, it did become a very important port for trade with Ireland (and troop shipments, too!).

In 1207, John granted a Charter to Liverpul, Leverepul, Lirpole — to present just a few examples of the wide variety of spellings to which it answered! This gave Liverpool the status of a free borough by the sea, and the town and port, although progressing slowly at first, never looked back. From this ancient recognition, the little borough eventually attracted great men (including some of the London merchants who settled here following the Plague and the Great Fire), whose business wisdom placed Liverpool irrevocably upon the global map of commerce.

The real prosperity and growth of this town and port had their foundations in the early trade with America and the slave trade. Liverpool became the number one port in the latter vile business. By 1800, Liverpool was handling ninety per cent of the world's slave trade and it was no wonder that the drunken tragedian, George Cooke, when hissed at and made fun of on stage in Liverpool one night, shouted back at the audience: "I have not come here to be insulted by a set of wretches, of which every brick in your infernal town is cemented with an African's blood!"

Scores of Liverpool ships sailed on the infamous slave-

3. Crowds gather for the Royal opening of the Queensway Tunnel by King George V in July 1934.

trade passages on a route known as 'the triangle'. They would leave the Mersey carrying cargoes of goods, like Lancashire and Yorkshire clothing, and knives, hatchets, guns, gunpowder and trinkets from Birmingham and Sheffield, out to West Africa in return for black slaves. The latter were crammed into the ships in appalling conditions, generally shackled and unable to move about. Thousands died and were cast overboard to feed the sharks as the vessels sailed across the Atlantic to the islands of the West Indies and the southern states of America. There, they would be exchanged for money or goods — generally tobacco, sugar, molasses and rum, which were carried back to Britain for more profit.

In spite of the prosperity this evil trade brought to the town, there were many fervent Liverpool abolitionists who spoke up and fought hard to stop it — men like William Roscoe and William Rathbone, distinguished men of distinguished families. But the slavers were die-hards and carried on their trade right up to 1 May 1807, the date that British participation in the trade was outlawed.

Between New Year's Day 1806, and 1 May 1807, 185 slave ships sailed out of Liverpool and carried 49,213 slaves. The slavers were determined to get their pound of flesh right up to the last day.

From the time of the Industrial Revolution, the Liverpool shipowners had really got to grips with world trade and with those in other professions, created one of the most important and thriving cities in the world.

Daniel Defoe, author of *Robinson Crusoe*, was enchanted by the town's layout and architecture, and on his second visit in 1690, found Liverpool: "much bigger than at my first seeing it." After his third visit, he found the town larger still, increasing in wealth, business and buildings and was moved to write: "What it may grow to in time, I know not."

But wait — old Liverpool was not always catching bouquets! Let us hear what American author, Nathaniel Hawthorne, thought of the port upon his arrival here in 1853 to take up his seven-year stint as US Consul: "Liverpool is a most detestable place as a residence that ever my lot was cast in — smoky, noisy, dirty, pestilential . . . The streets swarm with beggars by day and by night . . ."

Still, Liverpool has taken more slings and arrows than that in its stride.

Among the major 'firsts' for Liverpool was the creation of the first enclosed wet commercial dock, when Kent engineer, Thomas Steers, put flood-gates across the 'Pool' to keep vessels afloat at all stages of the tide.

This dock was opened in 1715 and there followed a long dock-building era in which Yorkshireman Jesse Hartley was the master builder. Engaged by the Corporation in 1824, Hartley was a tough and rugged man who swore and called a spade a spade. But many of the docks and quays that he built from Cyclopean blocks of granite still stand and operate today as a testimonial to his skill. Hartley was the sort of builder whom the Pharoahs would have employed to build their pyramids.

Standing supreme among Hartley's works is the Albert Dock complex — blocks of red brick and iron warehouses, built squarely around the enclosed dock of that name. Opened by Prince Albert, Queen Victoria's consort, in 1846, the dock and those adjoining it, were finally abandoned in 1972. They were left open to the river and they silted up; their gates rusted and rotting and their quaysides overgrown with grass and weeds. The warehouses were in a similar plight, completely derelict and decaying, all their windows broken and much of their brickwork damaged — all were scheduled for demolition.

They were painstakingly restored (even to the point of using some of the Victorian tools with which they were originally constructed), with all the original window spaces opened up and re-glazed, and with lead-coated steel roofs to match those with which Hartley had capped them.

The whole complex is now a maritime village and is Liverpool's jewel-in-the-crown of its tourist attractions. The complex comprises the largest collection of grade one listed buildings in Great Britain, accommodating specialist shops, restaurants, pubs, offices, exhibition and entertainment facilities. It also incorporates the popular *Tate of the North* gallery and the Merseyside Maritime Museum, which is fast becoming the world's best. Old Jesse would have been mighty proud of this admirable monument to his prowess.

The central feature of Liverpool's fine waterfront is the Pier Head with its trio of three grand buildings — the Royal Liver, Cunard and Port of Liverpool. Before them lies the Landing Stage, now considerably shorter than it used to be when it was the riverside doorstep to Liverpool, where millions of visitors from overseas landed from the famous liners of yesteryear.

Other wonderful buildings, like St George's Hall, the main Museum, the Central and Picton Libraries and the Walker Art Gallery, enrich the city's central area, which also boasts a huge, thriving shopping centre, drawing people from a wide area beyond Liverpool.

More magnificent still are the two giant Cathedrals, which overlook all of Merseyside from their elevated ridge twixt town and suburb.

Liverpool Cathedral, on St James' Mount and with a central tower rising 308 feet above floor level, is the Anglican Cathedral that was designed by Sir Giles Gilbert Scott, a Roman Catholic.

The RC Metropolitan Cathedral at Mount Pleasant, only a stone's-throw away and ultra modern with a cone-shaped base lantern tower and a central altar, was designed by Sir Frederick Gibberd, a Free churchman. These wonderful cathedrals — both completed this century, their foundation stones being laid in 1904 and 1933 respectively — are linked by a street called Hope. They are symbols of the firm and friendly Christian fellowship so evident on Merseyside today.

The world's first steam-hauled, passenger and freight railway — the Liverpool and Manchester Railway — began in Liverpool. Its famous engineer was George Stephenson, 'father' of railways, whose feat in laying it across marshy Chat Moss en route to Manchester, is still talked about among railway enthusiasts. This historic railway was opened in Liverpool on 15 September 1830 by the Duke of Wellington, then Prime Minister. This was a triumphal occasion for the town, but saddened later that day by the death of MP William Huskisson, who was run over by Stephenson's Rocket at Parkside, Golborne.

Twelve years later, Britain's first public baths and wash-house was opened in Liverpool — thanks to the commonsense and perseverance of that humble little woman, Kitty Wilkinson. She called attention to the need for washing facilities for the town's poor at a time of cholera

4. Birkenhead's Vittoria Dock during the Tall Ships Race, August 1984.

outbreaks.

In 1847 in a similar but professionally more elevated vein, Dr William Duncan became not only Liverpool's, but also the country's, first public health officer. Indeed, the city gave a lead to the rest of Britain in other 'first' aspects of health and public welfare like:- School for the Blind (1791); Provincial Children's Hospital (1851); District Nurse (1859); Provincial Nurses' School (1862); Slum Clearance Scheme (1864); Society for the Prevention of Cruelty to Children (1883); School of Tropical Medicine (1899); Tuberculosis Campaign (1901).

For countless years, Liverpool has embraced a strong tradition of culture and devotion to higher learning and it created fine institutions like the Athenaeum, the Lyceum, the Literary and Philosophical Society and the Royal Institution in the late eighteenth and early nineteenth centuries. It was, therefore, just a question of time, interest and money, but perhaps above all, local pride, before a college was founded in 1881. Then, in July 1903, the University of Liverpool was established by Royal Charter.

There are so many more historical and modern facets to lively Liverpool that justice cannot be done to all of them in this introduction. Further graphical chapters on people, places and events are opened up in the following pages, where a wealth of fine photographs and illustrations record more interesting occasions and highlights of the city — from the turn of the century to the present.

Volume 2 of *Bygone Merseyside* to follow, will contain another wide variety of fascinating pictures. These are books you will wish to keep.

5. above: Horse-drawn buses were still in general use when these single deck trams ran on suburban routes.

6. below: Horse cabs and 'toast-rack' trams at the Pier Head terminus c1900.

7. The Pier Head late 1940s with a goodview of the blitz-damaged city.

8. The Mersey plays rough between George's Landing Stage and the Pier Head, January 1948.

10. A fine view of the Overhead Railway and the central Goree warehouse from the Liver Building.

9. Liverpool water front with its fine buildings and the famous Liver Birds perched on their high twin towers, February 1982.

11. Goree Piazzas in May 1947, named after the island of Goree off the coast of West Africa. Legend has it that slaves were in chains here, but this is untrue. Washington Irving worked in the Goree in 1817 and Nathaniel Hawthorne, the American Consul in Liverpool, had an office there from 1853-57.

THE EXCHANGE LIVERPOOL

12. *above:* There have been three different sets of buildings called Exchange Buildings on this city site of Exchange Flags, at the rear of the Town Hall. Part of the property pictured was demolished just before the war and the remainder in 1949. The Nelson Monument survives.

13. *left:* June 1957 and Liverpool celebrates the 750th anniversary of its Royal Charter with a week of pageantry and special events. This was the scene outside the town hall where the band of the King's Regiment (Liverpool) played to the crowds awaiting the arrival of the Queen Mother.

14. *below:* Former Lord Mayors and Lady Mayoresses at a reunion dinner held at the town hall by the then Lord Mayor and Lady Mayoress, Alderman and Mrs Cowley, 1965-66.

15. The City Council in session at Liverpool's Regency Town Hall.

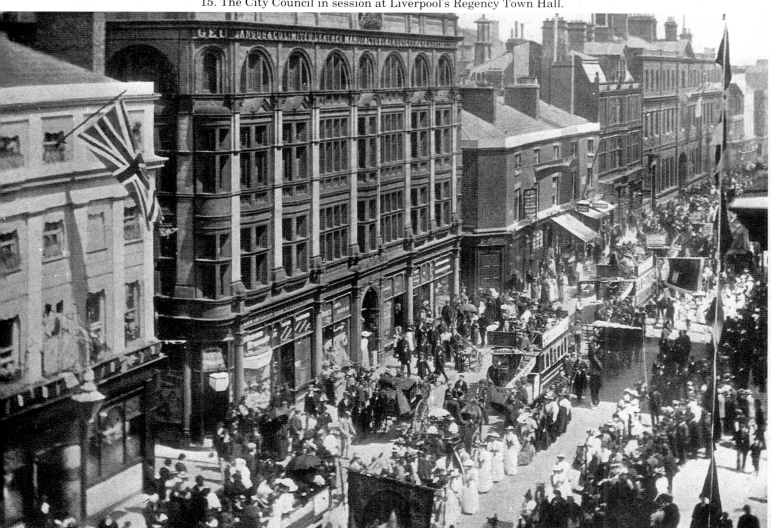

16. A gala day at the turn of the century. The procession, which appears to be composed of women, moves along Dale Street.

17. *above:* The old facade and forecourt of Central Station at the junction of Church Street and Ranelagh Street.
18. *below:* Lord Street c1903, looking towards the Pier Head.

19. The great fire at Henderson's Store on the corner of Lord Street and Whitechapel on 22 June 1960. It was Liverpool's biggest blaze since the blitz and claimed eleven lives.

20-21. Countless irreplaceable treasures were lost when Liverpool Museum was bombed and burned in May 1941. In the 1980s the museum's grand frontage remains the same but its interior has been completely redesigned and rebuilt.

22. The Walker Art Gallery was presented to the town by the Mayor, Alderman Andrew Barclay Walker, and opened by Lord Derby on 6 September 1877 — a day the town observed as a general holiday. The gallery forms the backdrop to this historic turn-of-the-century photograph in which a new electric tramcar can be seen with a horse-drawn tram.

23. *left:* Sculpture from 1751 to 1920 delights one of the many visitors viewing the gallery's permanent collection.

24. *below:* Children's work on show for the Kellogg's National Exhibition of Children's Art, March 1979.

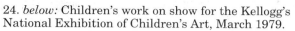

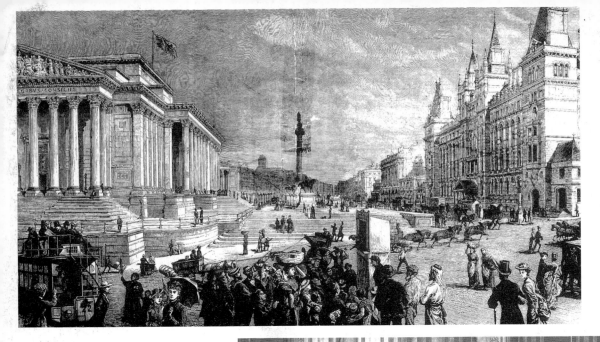

25. *left*: Classical-style St George Hall, founded in 1838 and pictured left in this fine old etching of Lime Street, has been described as one of the grander buildings in Britain. The Wellington Memorial column (*top centre*) and the former North Western Hotel block (*right*) still exist.

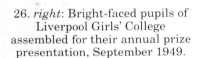

26. *right*: Bright-faced pupils of Liverpool Girls' College assembled for their annual prize presentation, September 1949.

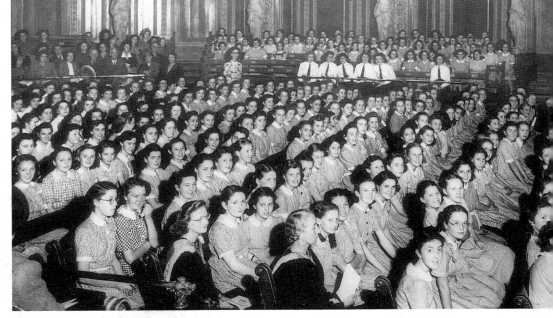

27. *left:* Many excellent music evenings and events have been held in the hall's lovely concert room.

28. *right:* The beautiful marble tile patterned floor in St George Hall, which is generally covered to preserve it. The focal point of this magnificent room is the famous Willis organ.

29-30. Sombre times on St George's Hall plateau. *above:* The huge rally during the transport workers' strike and riot of 1911. The event is remembered in Liverpool as Red (or, generally, 'Bloody') Sunday, when two men were shot and several others, including policemen, were injured. *below:* Troops deploy during the 1919 Police Strike. More than 3,000 troops were brought into the city and three warships were stationed in the Mersey.

31. *above:* King George V and Queen Mary at St George's Hall shortly before the King opened Gladstone Dock in July, 1927.

32. *below:* Liverpool National Fire Service (NFS) parade on the occasion of the second anniversary of the founding of the service. The NFS was disbanded in 1948 in favour of a return to fire brigades under local authority control.

33. Liverpool Cathedral Church of Christ from St James'
Cemetery, where quite a number of well-known Liverpool
characters are buried

34-36. *left:* One of the huge wooden pipes for the cathedral's organ being delivered in December 1923. The pipe was 32 feet long and weighed more than a ton. *right:* The wooden cross from the grave of an unknown soldier in Flanders is presented to Liverpool Cathedral by Major General Sir Fabian Ware at a British Legion service on 16 July 1931. *below:* Sunlight and shadow for the Liverpool College commemoration service in October 1931 conducted by Dr C M Chavasse.

37. *above:* The blitz. The cathedral escaped a near-miss at the price of residential property destroyed in St James Road.
38. *below:* A great deal of the cluttered property seen in this picture has now been swept away and the face of the town has changed considerably.

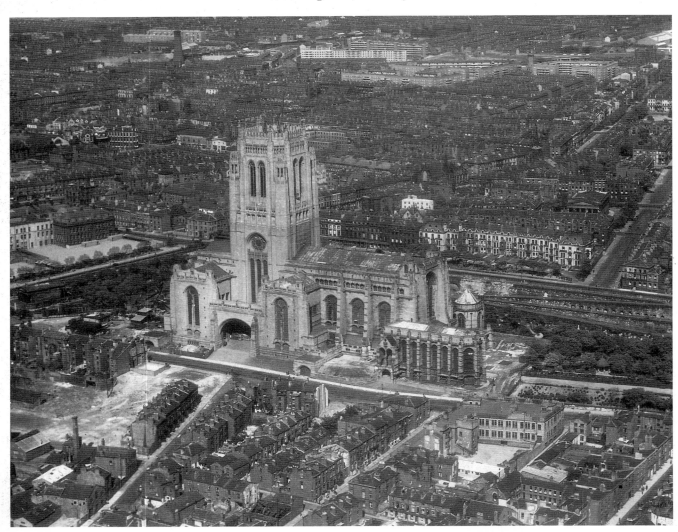

39. *above:* The nautical parade which followed the 1971 Battle of the Atlantic service at the cathedral.
40. *below:* A delightful portrait of dedicated wood-carver and stone-mason Thomas Murphy, pictured in January 1983 at the age of 78, while still working on the cathedral where he started in 1934.

41. *opposite page:* The Metropolitan Cathedral of Christ The King takes shape, a cocoon of scaffolding hiding the Lantern Tower.

42. *above:* The vaults of the proposed original cathedral after work had ceased because of the lack of funds. The new ultra-modern cathedral was built on the site.

43. *below:* The massive cone-shaped mainframe prior to the building of the Lantern Tower.

44. *right:* The Lantern Tower from within.

45. A priest firing a gun in a cathedral . . . ? In the cause of science Monsignor Cyril Taylor fires a pistol to test the acoustics, watched by resident architect Philip Harrison.

46. *below:* A superb view of the central altar, the focal point of the vast main floor. The altar was carved from a nineteen-ton block of flawless white marble and came from Skopje, Yugoslavia.

47. Nineteen ordinands prostrate themselves before the High Altar at this special service. They were the first to be ordained at the new cathedral — only a week after its consecration.

48. *below:* The beauty, dignity and simplicity of this modern cathedral clearly shows in this scene from the Celebration Mass to mark the anniversary of Archbishop Beck's twenty-five years as a Bishop.

49. *opposite right page:* A floodlit view of Liverpool's Anglican Cathedral which was officially lit up in a ceremony performed by the Chairman of the City Council, Hugh Dalton, and the Chairman of the County Council, Ben Shaw.

51. *right:* The spectacular effect created by the floodlighting of the Metropolitan Cathedral of Christ The King.

50. *below:* Looking towards the river from the University buildings, the city's two cathedrals dominate the skyline and are joined by a street called Hope.

52-53. Liverpool University's old red-brick Victorian building (*above*) contrasts sharply with the newer buildings of the modern university, which now take up many acres of the central city.

54-56. Liverpool has an abundance of beautiful parks and gardens. *above left:* Spring in Calderstones Park 1950. *above right:* Calderstones Park, May 1960. *below:* The floral clock in the children's garden, Stanley Park, 1936.

57. *above left:* Boating on Sefton Park lake in 1936.

58. *above right:* Morning visitors to Sefton Park stand and watch o of several model yachts being sailed by their owners, February 196

59. *below:* Yo-ho-ho and a bottle of rum! A pre-war photograph of Sefton Park's pirate ship *Jolly Roger*. She was built in 1928 as part of park pageant but sank in 1940 after becoming waterlogged.

60-61. Liverpool police in review at Sefton Park. *above:* The march past the Lord Mayor in May 1933. *below:* A Mayoral review of the city's mounted police in May 1938.

62. *above:* Thousands gathered in Sefton Park to hear *Echo and the Bunnymen.*
63. *below:* Thousands also gathered to attend an open-air service of the united church in the Liverpool International Garden Festival grounds on 7 May 1984, to celebrate the opening of the festival.

64-66. Out of a vast waterfront wilderness was created Liverpool's glorious 1984 International Garden Festival.
The large building in the above photographs is the Festival Hall.
below: The Japanese Garden — with real live exhibits!

67. *above:* Her Majesty Queen Elizabeth II opens the Festival.

68. *above:* There were even gardens within the Festival Hall. Here Mrs Ju
Hobson and her daughter Tracy throw coins in the water feature garden built
Douglas Knight of Formby.

69. *left:* Her Majesty meets BBC's *Blue Peter* star *Goldie* (with programme present
Simon Groom). *Goldie* appears to be appreciating the perfume of the Queen
flowers.

70-71. A festival of a different kind was the May Horse Parade, held regularly before the war and not revived until many years afterwards. Thousands would line the route taken by the procession of these magnificent animals.

72-76. Garlands, bunting and flowers. *above:* Pitt Street (Chinatown) during King George V's Silver Jubilee in 1935. *below left:* Loyal but poor, Thistle Terrace, King George VI's Coronation in 1937. *below right:* Claypole Street, Edge Hill, never looked so pretty. *opposite top:* Illuminated tram with band playing on the top deck tours the streets in celebration of King George VI's Coronation. *opposite bottom:* Pitt Street again, this time it's for the 1937 Coronation.

77-78. 1951 Festival of Britain. Festival dragons make their way along Brunswick Street and into Castle Street. Elsewhere it's street party time.

79. *above:* Warburton Street, Edge Hill, decorated for Queen Elizabeth's Coronation, June 1953.
80. *below:* Mums and dads take to the boards and stage a Coronation concert for the kids of Scarisbrick Road, Norris Green.

When the Queensway Tunnel was built as the under-Mersey road link between Liverpool and Birkenhead, some folk called it the Eighth Wonder of the Modern World.

Costing nearly £8 million and taking eight years and eight months to construct, this great feat of civil engineering ranked financially as the biggest single municipal enterprise ever undertaken in Britain. King George V, accompanied by Queen Mary (after whom the tunnel was named) opened it on 18 July 1934. The Mersey Railway Tunnel came first, though. This was officially opened in January, 1886, by the Prince of Wales, who became King Edward VII. It was the first under-water railway and also Britain's first to be converted from steam to electric traction. Tunnelling for Queensway began in Liverpool on 16 December 1925, and from Birkenhead on 10 March 1926. On 3 April 1928, the Lord Mayor of Liverpool and the Mayor of Birkenhead (suitably clad for the dark and wet experience at this stage) shook hands as the breakthrough was made. The pilot headings joined together with, at the most, only 2.9 cm divergence of alignment, showing the accuracy of the survey work and correct determination of working levels.

With a diameter of 44 feet, the four-lane tunnel, with its approaches and two dock branches, is 2.87 miles long. Some 1,200,000 tons of rock, gravel and clay were excavated and usefully employed in the construction of Otterspool Prom-enade, land reclamation at Dingle and as a filling for a worked-out quarry at Storeton, Birkenhead. It is lined with 82,000 tons of cast-iron and 270,000 tons of concrete.

To commemorate the opening of Queensway, 150,000 local schoolchildren were given a medal — thousands of which are undoubtedly still cherished by families today.

Liverpool's second Mersey road tunnel—Kingsway, so-named by the Queen in honour of her late father, King George VI — was opened by her on 24 June 1971. About a mile nearer the estuary than Queensway and linking the city with Wallasey, it was built to cope with the ever-increasing Merseyside traffic that was causing regular rush-hour jams.

A pick-and-shovel brigade of hundreds of men — and 560,000 pounds of explosives — carved out Queensway Tunnel. But a huge and powerful boring machine, called the 'Mole', cut the twin, two-lane tunnels of Kingsway, where the first breakthrough was made on 4 March 1970. Tube No 2, still being bored when the Queen opened No 1, was not opened to traffic until 13 February 1974.

81-82. *above:* The Tunnel Pageant in Castle Street, July 1934. Liverpool held a week of celebrations to commemorate the opening of the tunnel, including a ceremony of remembrance held at the Cenotaph on St George's Hall plateau and attended by thousands of citizens and ex-servicemen and women. *below:* Part of the drained old George's Dock being prepared for a visit by the Princess Royal who, on 16 December 1925, started the drills for sinking the first 200 ft deep vertical shaft of the Queensway Tunnel.

83. *above:* This scene, like some game about to begin, shows the pneumatic drills ready to chatter at a Royal command.

84. *right:* Getting ready for the breakthrough. The pilot tunnels joined together only 2.9cm out of alignment, proving the accuracy of the survey work and correct determination of working levels.

85. *below:* Excavation of the pilot headings which were a bit larger than some of the London Underground tunnels.

G-1 MERSEY TUNNEL
Contract No. 1, May 11th, 1928.
RENDEL ST. HEADING.

86. *above:* The Lord Mayor of Liverpool, the Mayors of Birkenhead and Wallasey and thirty foreign consuls based at Liverpool tour the workings in December 1929.

87. *below:* A party of 200 men, including the Lord Mayor of Liverpool (Mr Lawrence Holt), other local mayors, council members and engineers, toured the full length of the tunnel on 9 September 1930.

THE MERSEY TUNNEL — 6th May 1933.
Lining Interior Surface of Tunnel with Astroplex.

88-90. *left:* The Duke of York visits the workings. *above:* Completing a Herculean task — lining the tunnel's interior surface with special plaster — by hand! *below:* Historic moment as King George V (*standing*) opens the tunnel. Queen Mary, in white, is on the left. The royal couple then motored through the tunnel to Birkenhead.

91-93. In building the second Mersey Tunnel (Kingsway), engineers were faced with a big problem when a major fault of shattered rock was found some 1,200 feet from the Wallasey shore. This new crossing was the first large underwater tunnel to be designed for boring by a machine, creating yet another milestone in the history of Merseyside and also in the records of tunnel construction. However work was forced to come to a halt until the problem of the fault was resolved.

The artist's impression shows the problem, which was ultimately solved by constructing an 'umbrella' of reinforced concrete to bridge the fault and the Mole was able to progress

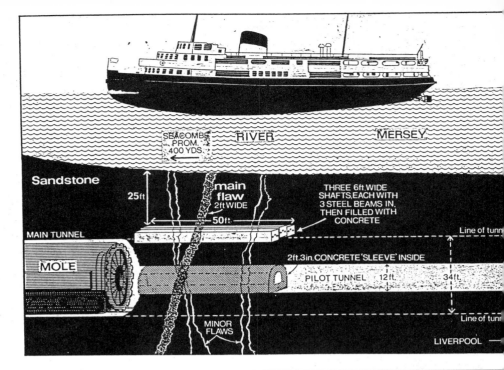

The mighty Mole (*below*), which cut the twin Kingsway tunnels, was the largest tunnel-boring machine in the world. Built in Pakistan by an American-owned firm it was 45 feet long, weighed 350 tons and carried a crew of eighteen to twenty men. The Mole had already successfully bored five tunnels before coming to Merseyside without the need for preliminary pilot tunnels. On arrival, the Mole had to be modified, with the cutting head reduced to 33 feet 11 inches and a hole provided in the head to allow access to the pilot tunnel. *right:* The 'flaw' point where the Mole had to stop.

94-95. Her Majesty Queen Elizabeth II opens the Kingsway Tunnel. *above:* The Queen's Colour of The King's (Liverpool) Regiment is dipped in salute. *below:* Big smiles from the spectators as the Queen 'goes walkabout'.

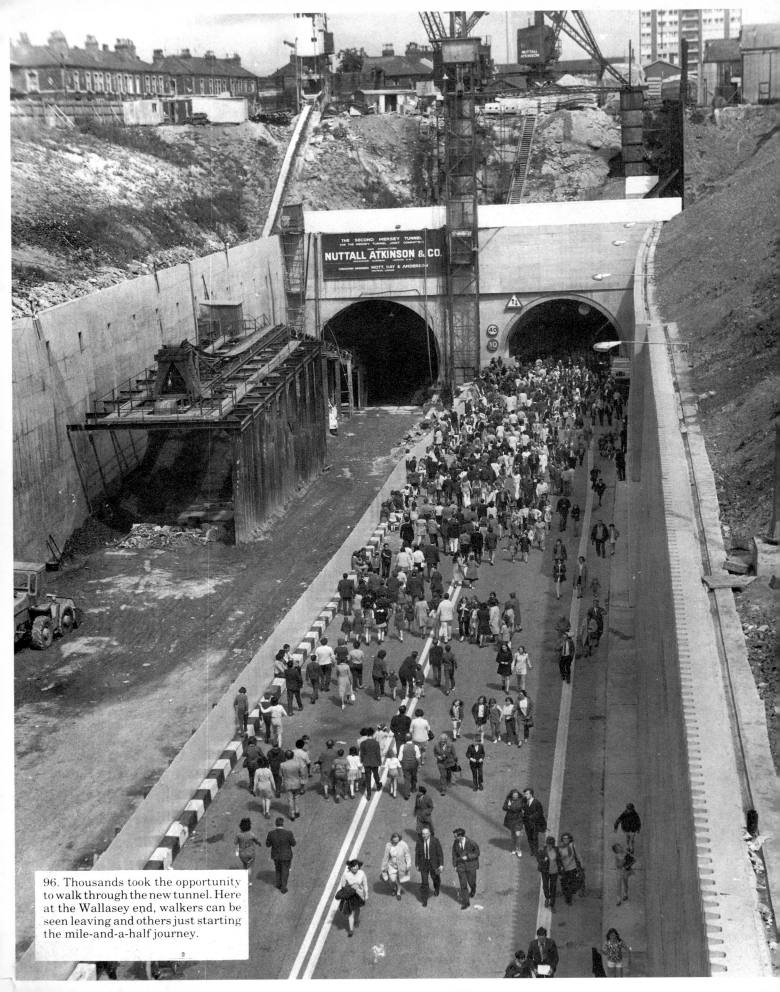

THE SECOND MERSEY TUNNEL
FOR THE MERSEY TUNNEL JOINT COMMITTEE
MAIN CONTRACTORS
NUTTALL ATKINSON & CO.
CONSULTING ENGINEERS MOTT, HAY & ANDERSON

96. Thousands took the opportunity to walk through the new tunnel. Here at the Wallasey end, walkers can be seen leaving and others just starting the mile-and-a-half journey.

There were 'ferries across the ersey' for hundreds of years before nger Gerry Marsden sang their aises!

No doubt, vessels of some escription carried folk from bank to ank even in Roman times, but ferry rvices proper began with the monks Birkenhead as early as the thirteenth ntury when they were granted the rry rights in 1282.

It was 2d for a horseman and a rthing for a pedestrian in those days d many were the complaints when e charges rose to one halfpenny for ch foot passenger and one penny for man and whatever he could carry!

The ferry services thrived and grew d eventually passed out of private ands to be run by the local authorities Birkenhead and Wallasey.

Earlier this century there were as any as eight piers on the Cheshire ank of the Mersey — at New Brighton, gremont, Seacombe, Woodside, ranmere, Rock Ferry, New Ferry and astham.

Hundreds of millions of passengers ere carried on these busy cross-river utes during the heyday of the ferries, it these figures have been amatically reduced since the last ar with the advent of the family car, e two road tunnels and, of course, the odated electric underground railway.

. top right: Paddle-steamer ferries Liverpool's George's Landing stage about 1890.

. centre right: The ferry *Overchurch* as to compete with hefty ice floes ring one of the big freezes. The ersey has frozen over completely in ry severe winters.

. bottom: A picture that encapsulates e 'romance' of the Mersey — the oyal Daffodil about to tie up at orge's Landing.

100. The *Wallasey*, built in 1927, was a well-known Mersey ferry-boat, serving for 36 years.

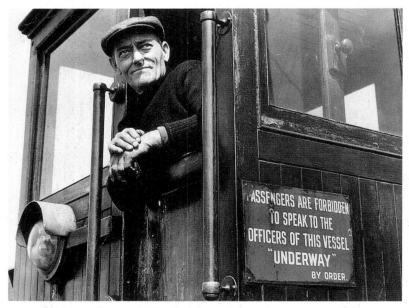

101. So now you know!

102. The plaque commemorating the exploits of the ferry-boat *Daffodil* which, as HMS *Daffodil IV*, took part in the bloody battle of Zeebrugge with her sistership HMS *Iris*, in 1918. Both ferries were later accorded the honour of the prefix *Royal* — by command of His Majesty King George V.

103-104. Ferry-boat cruises are always a good excuse for a dance — officially like the one above on the *Royal Iris,* or simply an inspired solo knees-up like the one below.

105. *left:* Calm and warm, hardly a ripple from the flag . . . it's a lovely day for a cruise and some quiet contemplation on the *Royal Iris.*

106. *below:* Part of the big crowd of trippers anxious to get seats on the ferry to New Brighton on a sunny day in June 1962.

107. *opposite top:* The other face of the Mersey. But it has to be rougher than this to prevent the ferries from maintaining their services. The *Leasowe* passes a low-lying tanker battling with the waves. February 1967.

108. *opposite bottom:* Great skill is called for by the master and his crew in the regular berthing of ferries in stormy weather.

109. The *St Tudno*, pictured here with the Cunarder *Carinthia* astern, was a very popular little cruise ship. She and her sisters, like the *St Seiriol* and *St Elvies*, sailed regularly from Liverpool on cruises to North Wales, calling at places like Llandudno, Bangor and Menai Bridge.

110.*left:* Holidaymakers enjoying a cruise on the *St Tudno*.

111. This is the kind of glorious scenery they saw in the Menai Straits, where *St Tudno* is seen homeward bound in September 1934.

112-113. Liverpool is still the traditional UK shipping gateway to Ireland and the Isle of Man. Thousands used to flock down to Prince's Landing Stage for trips to the Isle of Man and these pictures taken in May 1959 and August 1956 respectively show how popular these sailings were. At peak holiday times, like July and August, extra boats had to be brought into service.

114-115. *opposite page:* Flashback to June 1966 and vessels are laid up in the north docks due to the seamen's strike. How many Blue Funnel ships are there? *this page:* Gladstone Dock container berth in 1969, built as an interim measure while the Seaforth terminal was constructed.

116. *opposite page:* Derelict and silted up, the Albert Dock complex of yesterday. Following restoration, Albert Dock today forms a popular maritime village, full of specialist shops, pubs, restaurants and more.

117. *right*: Merseyside Maritime Museum now occupies a number of quays, water areas, other small buildings and floating exhibits in addition to this giant 'Hartley' warehouse block and dockside.

118. A popular entertainment centre, almost anything goes at the Albert Dock. This was the firework extravaganza when the rock group *Frankie Goes To Hollywood* hit town in July 1986.

119. Albert Dock market stalls, August 1988.

120. *overleaf*: The revitalised Albert Dock complex.

121-122. Forests of masts and spars like this had not been seen on the Mersey for about a century but for four magical days in August 1984, Merseyside played host to the participants of the Tall Ships' Race.

123. A big hand for all the visiting crews as they start
their parade through the city. Some sixty square-riggers, schooners, barques and more had put into the docks on both sides of the river to turn the clock back to the days of sail.

124. *right:* Swedish schooners *Gladan* (*left*) and *Falken* rest in the quietude of Canning Dock on arrival

125. *left:* Just a fraction of the estimated one million people who gathered on both banks of the Mersey to bid the ships farewell.

126. Her Majesty Queen Elizabeth II waves to a passing Tall Ship as Prince Andrew prepares to take a picture.

127. *Gorch Foch* sails past the *Britannia*.

128. The *Sagres* heads for home.

129. *left:* The jolly crew of the Bermuda Ketch, *Thalassea*.

131. *opposite page:* A view that sums up the 'core' of Merseyside — Birkenhead in the foreground and Liverpool a ferry ride away.

130. *below:* High on the yards of their giant ship, the *Kruzenshtern*, Russian sailors salute the Queen. After jolly, fun-filled days for visitors and crews, the Tall Ships all put to sea again in the great Parade of Sail and headed for home. They were sorry to depart, but Merseyside will be more than happy to meet them all again — for they are due to return in August 1992, for another grand finale in Liverpool.

Liverpool without Birkenhead just would not be the same place. They have virtually grown up together.

The monks of Birkenhead Priory linked the two towns by ferry as early as 1150 and today they are joined (with Wallasey, too) by three busy tunnels (one train, two traffic), as explained within this book. Although divided by the broad River Mersey, together the towns form the hub of Merseyside. Geographically, Liverpool is like half a wheel, with its main routes converging on the Pier Head like spokes. Birkenhead, with Wallasey, on the lovely Wirral Peninsular, more or less complete the circle! Indeed, in the last war, when Merseyside was bombed regularly for about nineteen months, Germany always regarded Liverpool and Birkenhead (and, of course, Bootle, which is contiguous with the city) as one major target area. We all suffered together!

Like Liverpool, Birkenhead owes it foundation to its maritime industry, boasting 182 acres of docks, which were very busy in their heyday. Two historic characters helped to put this town on the map. They were John Laird, son of William, the founder of the famous shipbuilder's, who has been described as 'the father of Birkenhead', and Lord Leverhulme, the soap-maker, whose 'workers village' of Port Sunlight, founded in 1889, is a showpiece which attracts visitors from all over the world.

Laird's was founded as an ironworks in 1842 and eventually became Cammell Laird. Today, it is known as Vickers Shipbuildings and Engineering, Limited, part of one of the world's major shipbuilding organisations.

It was John Laird who pioneered iron shipbuilding in Britain and the company constructed many famous ships and had war records second to none.

Mention of the Mersey's Wirral bank without New Brighton would be unforgivable. This jolly little seaside resort, perched on the tip of the peninsular at the confluence of the river and Liverpool Bay, is fondly embraced by Merseyside.

Thousands of older folk from the city (and the industrial towns of Lancashire and beyond) hold cherished memories of New Brighton when a 6d ferry trip from Liverpool released them from their daily life in smoke and grime, and often abject poverty, to enjoy a happy day's outing, with clean sea breezes and lots of fun.

The ferries may no longer call at New Brighton, whose pier has been demolished, but cars and public transport are now returning the crowds to breath new life into this historical Merseyside resort.

Some interesting pictures of the Wirral bank — which Liverpudlians have always called 'over the water' — follow. And there will be lots more in Volume 2 of *Bygone Merseyside*.

132. Wallasey's 1967 Festival of Sport, in Birkenhead's West Float, is temporarily halted when the big ships have priority.

133. Loading steel pipes for China at Birkenhead docks.

134. Giant gates from Birkenhead's Alfred Dock
undergoing overhaul in 1960.

135. Towing tugs are dwarfed by the immense oil rig,
Sovereign Explorer

136. Merchantmen manoeuvre for docking at Birkenhead in January, 1937.

137. Woodside Ferry (Birkenhead) as it looked in 1814.

138. Springtime in Hamilton Square, Birkenhead.

139. Low tide at New Brighton in June, 1960.

140. New Brighton Pier passenger bridge damaged by a storm in January, 1962.

141. New Brighton Pier, closed in 1972 and later demolished.

142. A birds-eye view from New Brighton across the river to Seaforth and Waterloo.

143. New Brighton's once-famous Tower, which rose 600 feet from the amusement park, was built in 1898 and dismantled in 1921.

144. Minus its giant tower but still impressive, this red-brick building accommodated a huge ballroom and provided for countless shows and exhibitions.

145. New Brighton Bathing Pool, with seating for 10,000, pictured shortly after its official opening by Lord Leverhulme in June 1934, when it was the world's largest swimming pool.

146. Water way of cooling off in the June
     heat of 1947!

147. Fort Perch Rock, New Brighton, is now a museum.

148. Modern Marines attack the fort — in training.

149. Stormy seas attack Fort Perch Rock.

150. Ships are built 'indoors' these days. Here's a submarine in the making.

151. Cammell Laird's modern shipyard at Birkenhead.

152. Destroyer HMS *Campbeltown* on the stocks and ready for launching.

153. Sections of the *Mauretania*'s engines being installed in Laird's machine-shop, December 1938.

154. The lads who make ships . . . men of Cammell Laird's 'knocking off' in January 1946, not long after their splendid wartime building and repairing record.

155. 'Mighty *Maurie*' (the 2nd) tunes up her engines for the first time as she is towed out of the shipyard, where she was built, May 1939.

156. The 'ark' graces the Mersey.

157-9. Famous aircraft carrier, *Ark Royal* (also the second) is launched at Laird's by the Queen in May, 1950.